People Jesus Met

Contents

Getting started	Learning Together, Large Visual Aids, Drama, Children's Needs	2
The enormous catch of fish	Jesus Calls His First Disciples	8
Jesus at the home of his friends	Jesus Helps Simon's Mother-in-law	11
The man let down through the roof	Jesus Offers Forgiveness and Healing	16
Jesus at a wedding	Jesus Changes Water into Wine	19
Matthew's special guest	Jesus Asks a Tax Collector to Follow Him	23
Why Zacchaeus climbed a tree	Jesus Welcomes Zacchaeus	25
Only one said thank you	Jesus Heals Ten Lepers	28
Meeting Jesus	Jesus Restores Bartimaeus' Sight	31
The little girl who got better	Jesus Heals an Official's Daughter	34
The man beside the pool	Jesus Brings Healing to a Crippled Man	37
Bibliography	Songs, Books and Useful Addresses	40

Thanks to everyone who has made this possible, especially Ruth End, Keith Brigham and my husband David

BOOK 3

Getting Started

Welcome to PEOPLE JESUS MET – a book of resource material, songs, stories, visual aids and activities to use in your toddler groups, pram services, family days and even (with a little bit of thought) family services.

All of this material is based on the idea of parents and children learning together. In this book we offer you 10 sessions all on the theme "People Jesus Met":

- Jesus Calls His First Disciples
- Jesus Helps Simon's Mother-in-law
- Jesus Offers Forgiveness and Healing
- Jesus Changes Water into Wine
- Jesus Asks a Tax Collector to Follow Him
- Jesus Welcomes Zacchaeus
- Jesus Heals Ten Lepers
- Jesus Restores Bartimaeus' Sight
- Jesus Heals an Official's Daughter
- Jesus Brings Healing to a Crippled Man

We have tried to start from a child's needs, emotions, interests, and from their world, which is centred around family and immediate neighbourhood. We hope that this material will help both parents and children to learn something of the joy of knowing Jesus.

Please note that, for each book, copying of templates and instructions is limited to their use with a group of up to ten children.

Learning together

All the ideas that follow are based on the aim of parents and children working together. They have been tried and tested with our own group, a place where parents welcome their friends and neighbours, where church baptism links are followed up, and where parents are helped to keep the promises they made at their child's baptism.

If you are using this material to lead a group of your own, you might find the following helpful.

❶ Arrive early, preferably with helpers, to set up the room and activity. Welcome people as they arrive.

❷ *About 20-25 minutes:*
- Welcome
- Singing
- Story with big visual aid
- Prayer - to conclude the story
- Craft activity

❸ *About 30-35 minutes:*
- Free time together with coffee, orange juice and toys
- Tidy up toys
- Closing prayer

❹ Tidy the room and leave it as you found it.

A one-hour session should give plenty of time to talk together and get to know each other. You will have already broken the ice while doing the activity as everybody tried to stop their children glueing their fingers to whatever they were making!

Don't panic!

You might feel a bit intimidated by all of this, but don't be, it is all here to help. This material is yours now. Have fun, and adapt it for your situation. Enjoy learning together.

Making a large visual aid

When you are thinking about large visual aids think BIG. Ask yourself if 4 or 5 children can play with it at once after you have used it, or as they use it. This means making it strong enough to withstand being played with and will also ensure it shouldn't collapse during story time.

Making large visual aids also means thinking ahead and collecting your materials in good time. If you need large boxes from shops be sure to ask well before you need them and explain why you want them. People are often only too keen to help with a toddlers' group.

There is a story about a man who made an aeroplane in his front room and then had to take it apart to get it out of the house. Where will you make your visual aids? Do you have enough room at home, and if you do, are you able to transport it to your meeting place? It might be easier to make it where you are going to use it, in which case, leave plenty of time before the session. Here are instructions for making the three large visual aids you will need later in this book.

Boat

You will need:
- 3 large apple boxes
- a square(ish) box about half the size of the apple boxes
- 4 or 5 A2 sheets of brown card
- parcel tape/stapler/PVA glue
- a good pair of heavy scissors

What to do:

❶ Stick the three apple boxes together along the long sides using parcel tape or stapler.

❷ Stick the smaller box at one end to make the back of the boat.

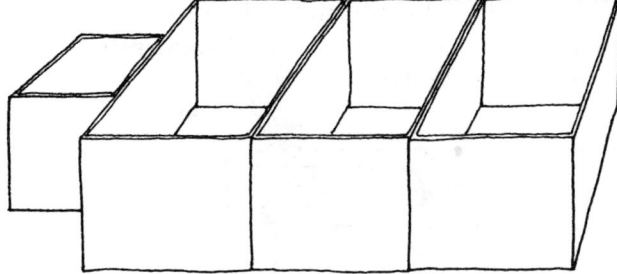

❸ Cut the brown card into lengths 42cm by 30cm checking first that this will cover the sides of your boxes.

❹ Stick the brown card along the sides of the apple boxes and curve it round the back of the boat. At the front of the boat curve the card to a point.

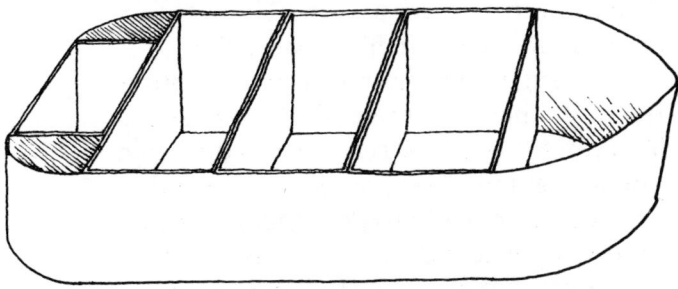

☞ *Use whichever method of sticking you prefer, parcel tape, stapler or glue. You might want to add a sail.*

Sycamore tree

You will need:
- a large cardboard tube at least 10cm diameter and 120cm tall from a carpet warehouse, or from a fabric shop where roller blinds are sold
- brown paper
- 2 or 3 A2 sheets of green card
- sellotape
- PVA glue and spreader
- thicker cardboard from supermarket boxes
- dark green paper or real sycamore leaves

What to do:

❶ Cover the tube in brown paper unless it is brown already. Bind 3 or 4 thinner tubes together if you could only get thinner tubes.

❷ Sellotape together some of the A2 sheets of green card according to the size of your tree and its proportions relative to the trunk.

❸ Draw the shape onto the card and cut it out. Cut a hole about 30cm diameter in the leaves, and 2 slits in the bottom so that the top part of the tree will slide onto the tube.

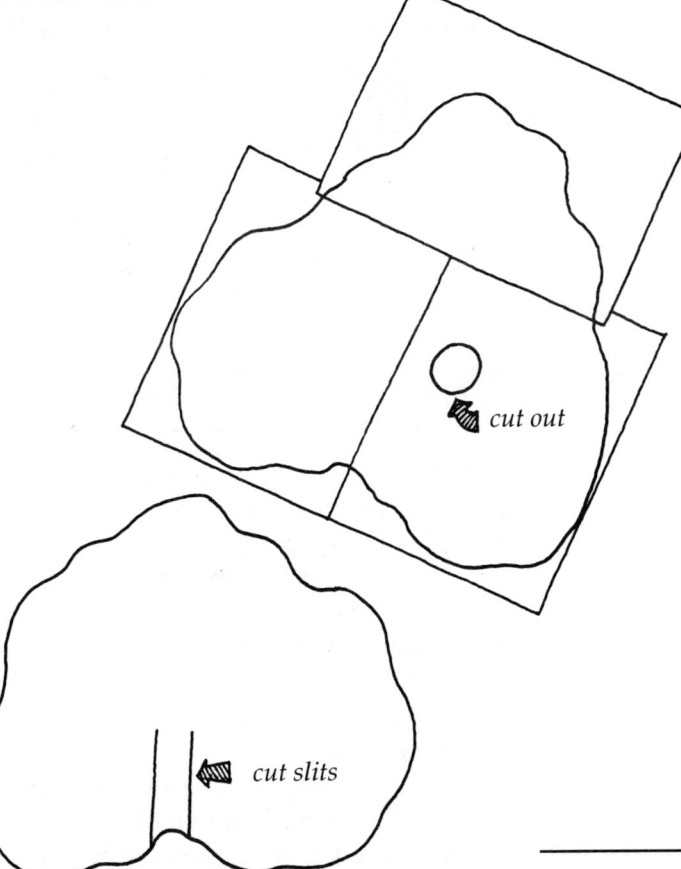

❹ Reinforce the green card with some thicker cardboard.

❺Cover the top part of the tree with real sycamore leaves or with paper leaf shapes cut out of green paper. Leave the hole clear to enable Zacchaeus to look through.

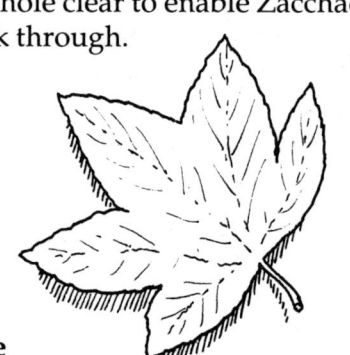
cover in leaves

House
You will need:
- cardboard box large enough to hold a freezer or washing machine
- a Stanley knife
- parcel tape

What to do:
❶If the box has flaps on both ends, cut them off the top and turn it upside-down.
❷Cut out a door on one side of the box, remembering to keep it attached on one side to make a hinge.
❸Cut out some windows on the other sides. Make them round, square, triangular or whatever shape you like.

cut off flaps

❹Cut a hole in the roof large enough for the man to get through but leave at least 20cm round it or you will severely weaken the house.

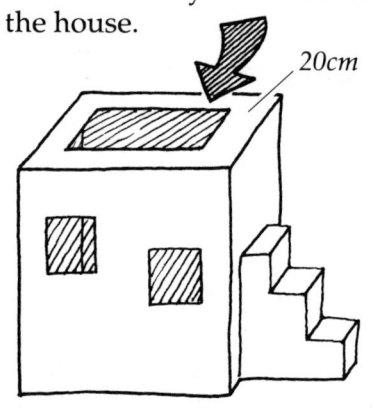
20cm

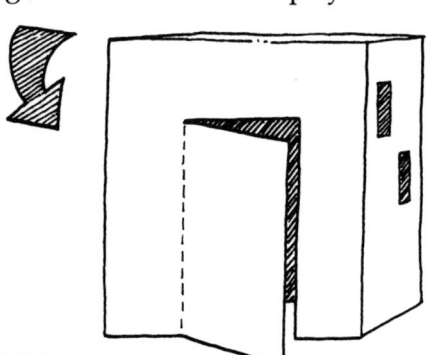

Drama

Let's start with two questions. Do you join in with action songs and rhymes? Do you play imaginary games with your children, pretending that you are going to the moon or that you are a sick patient in a hospital bed, or whatever they come up with? If the answer to either or both of these is yes, then you know what we mean by drama.

Drama is a super way of involving a child in the story. From an early age children imitate what they see happening around the home, or they act out different characters such as nurses, racing drivers, etc. Children like to copy. This gives us an opportunity to involve them in stories.

In the story of Zacchaeus, children can be part of the crowd; and in "The enormous catch of fish" they are the fishermen; in "The man let down through the roof" they take the part of the friends. You can tell the children what to do while you are telling the story. You may need someone else ready to help them, but by involving the children and stimulating their imaginations, they will get a great deal more out of the story and they will probably remember it better too. It will also help to keep their attention.

We have used other dramatic effects in

the two previous books in the series. Asking the children to make sound effects or join in with actions gets them involved, while using puppets and props can add an element of drama and catch the children's attention in a different way.

The storyteller can act out a part in the story, with just a very simple costume, sometimes just a hat or headscarf. Know your story well and practise where actions and sounds come in. Remember the children and parents want you to succeed. Drama is very versatile and a lot of fun. Enjoy exploring it with your group.

*S*tarting with the needs of a child...

In our opening paragraph we talk about how we try to start from a child's needs, emotions and interests and from their world which is centred around their family and immediate neighbourhood. Here we look a little closer at this and show how we have kept this in mind to try to provide you with appropriate material and patterns for working with your group.

The Group
Children and parents need to feel that they belong and are loved in a group. We should make sure we know them by name, welcome them, and spend time with them. We should listen to them and talk to them about the things that matter to them: a child's new shoes, illness in the family, sleepless nights.

Try to include an opportunity for finger rhymes, action songs, and clapping, so that babies are also involved as part of the group.

The Session
Children appreciate variety and in our sessions we need to remember that children (in particular) have only a short attention span. The programme needs to be fast moving and varied (see Learning Together) but the variety must also have familiar elements in it, or children and parents can easily become confused about what is going to happen next.

Hands play an important part in a child's development. Children of three months play with their hands; by six months they are picking things up and joining in the singing with bells and rattles; by two or three years they are playing drums and tambourines.

Small children benefit from the opportunity to be with and play with others even if they are playing alone with others around them. In "The enormous catch of fish" they try their hand at fishing the fish out of the pond with a rod and magnet alongside others. In Book 2 (*Stories Jesus Told*, CPAS 1991) we play Simon Says. When we sing "Everyone matters to Jesus" everyone claps and jumps if they are wearing particular colours. In all of these it is hoped that the children relate to one another even if playing alone.

We can also relate our stories to the child's environment. For example in Book 2 one of the stories is told through the eyes of two children, Matthew and Daniel. Children are also excited by parties, so it is easy for them to get caught up in "Jesus at the wedding" when the story involves a wedding party, or in the story of Matthew when the story involves getting ready for a party. In "The friends who helped" we talk about the different types of houses that the children live in. Another story in Book 2 uses animals as the main characters. This is something that children are very used to from their story books and television.

Children want to please, and they want to share their experiences. The activity time is another occasion to reinforce children and parents working together, learning skills, folding, sticking, colouring, glueing, etc. and then there is the important value of the activity as something to take home. For a joint activity to be successful it has to be enjoyed by both parents and children.

Showing our love for Jesus, sharing our experience of having Jesus as our friend and Lord is very important and we hope that children and their parents will respond to this.

Using the activity sheets

Read through the activity sheet well before you come to use it. This gives you time for forward planning (or you might find yourself having to collect forty toilet rolls in a week...). The sheet itself has been divided up into four sections:
- You will need
- Prepare in advance
- Get the room ready
- What each child/parent does.

You will need
This lists all the material you will need for the activity. This is where it is most important to think ahead. Ask the parents in your group as well as other members of the church congregation.

Prepare in advance
You have now gathered together everything you need for a particular session. What next? This section talks about the specific things that you need to do to get the activity ready.

Use old cereal packets for your templates. They are cheap, and will withstand repeated drawing around. Splash out on a good pair of scissors, with long blades.

The individual preparation instructions are fairly straightforward. You will usually need one set of activity pieces per child, plus a few extra.

Once all the bits and pieces are cut out, group them together in separate bags to take to the session.

Make up an activity yourself before the session. It will help you to explain how to make it, and to have "one you made earlier" to show the group.

Get the room ready
The sheet will tell you what each child needs to make the activity. In the centre of the table put things like glue, spreaders, pencils, etc. You can use the lids from 2- or 4-litre ice cream tubs as trays for things. When you are using PVA glue put a small amount in a plastic (not glass) tub. If your tubs have lids you can keep it from session to session. With PVA glue, always use spreaders as brushes get all clogged up. Pritt might seem easier, but it doesn't stick so well. Once PVA is stuck, it is stuck. Make sure you have enough glue spreaders to prevent children getting bored while they wait their turn.

If the activity needs sellotape, cut out the strips beforehand and stick them around an ice cream container lid. This avoids the need to have scissors out.

What each child/parent does
Show a completed activity to everybody, and explain one step at a time what you have to do to make one. Ask for questions, and be ready to help anyone with problems. (If you have a child under three it might be helpful to have someone looking after him or her while you explain it.)

Once the activity is made, ask mums or dads to write each child's name on the one they have made. They are often wet afterwards so leave them on the tables to dry.

Tidy up afterwards...
Have fun!

☞ *All measurements are given in cm (one inch is approximately 2.5 cm). Paper sizes (A2, 3, 4 and 5) follow the standard sizes.*

A2
42.0 x 59.4

A3
29.7 x 42.0

A4
21.0 x 29.7

A5
14.8 x 21.0

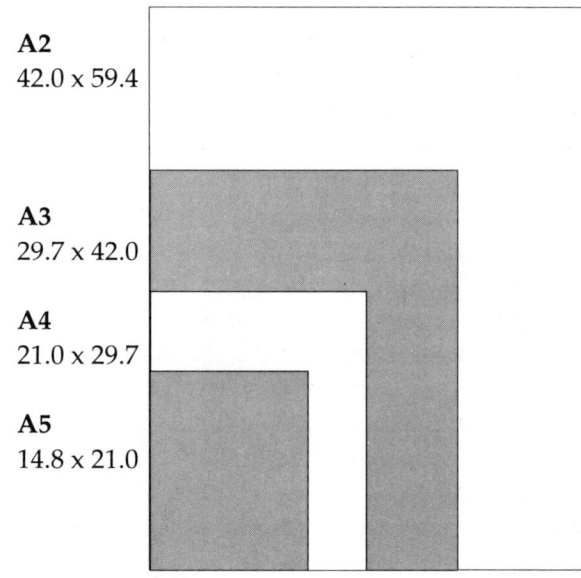

Can you think of someone who has been a great influence on you? Maybe you can think of several. Or perhaps there is someone you met only once, but who made a great, and lasting, impression.

As we look at this group of people that Jesus met we shall see something of the influence that he had on them and something of the impression that he made on them. We can think of Zacchaeus whose encounter with Jesus leaves him almost a different person. We can read of the time that Jesus called the first disciples, their meeting with him changing their lives in ways that they cannot have imagined in advance. The encounters are all different. Jesus doesn't work to a single blueprint. In his healings he heals some with a word or a command, like the man at the pool; some he heals with touch, like the official's daughter or Peter's mother-in-law.

Similarly people respond to him in different ways. Remember the nine lepers who do not come back, as well as Matthew the tax collector who follows him.

We hope you enjoy using **People Jesus Met** and as you use it you might meet with something of Jesus, as he meets others and touches their lives. Enjoy learning together!

BOOK 3 UNIT 1

The enormous catch of fish

Jesus Calls His First Disciples Luke 5:1-11

How would you feel if someone you had never met before came and told you how to do your job? This happens to Peter in verse 4, but see how he responds in verse 5. Why do you think he does this? Do you think it is something to do with the way he has heard Jesus speaking already? What does verse 6 tell us about the consequence of Peter obeying what Jesus tells him? What response does Peter make to Jesus in verse 8? What do they leave behind in verse 11?

Tell the story

Introduction:
The children can try fishing in the "pond" using their magnetic fishing rods. Explain that when people go out fishing in boats they use large nets to catch the fish.

Story:
Begin the story by setting the scene:

❶ Jesus had been teaching all morning and now the crowds had gone away.
❷ Jesus tells Simon to go fishing.
❸ Simon tells Jesus that they had fished all night, and they'd caught nothing, but he will do what Jesus tells him. They go out fishing.
❹ Now put 2 children in the "boat" and get them to throw out the net. (See page 3 for instructions on how to make the boat.) Get the other children to fill the net up with the brightly coloured fish, and fold it over so that the children in the boat can pull it in.
❺ Continue telling the story while the "drama" is being played out. It is such a large catch that they need help to pull it in. Get 2 other children to help.
❻ Conclude by saying that because of this 4 men left their jobs to follow Jesus around the countryside.
❼ Sing "Peter and James and John in a sailboat".

☞ *You might want to let the children play catching fish in the free play/coffee time (under supervision!)*

Theme
Jesus is someone we listen to.

Let's sing!
- " Who's the king of the jungle? "
- " Have you seen the pussycat? "
- " Big man "
- " Peter and James and John in a sailboat "

Activity
Make a stained glass window fish.

Visual aids
☆ a large boat made out of large cardboard boxes, big enough for 2 to 4 children
☆ a large net, old net curtains or onion bags
☆ some fish cut out of old magazine paper or sugar paper with a paper clip attached or staple through them
☆ some fishing rods made of sticks with a piece of string and a small magnet at the end of the string
☆ a "pond" consisting of a plastic bowl or baby bath with some paper fish in

Helpful resources
" The Lion Book of Stories of Jesus " (section 8)

Stained glass window fish

BOOK 3

UNIT 1

Prepare in advance
❶ Cut out the fish template using lines marked A.
❷ Using the template cut out in black card half the fish shapes required.

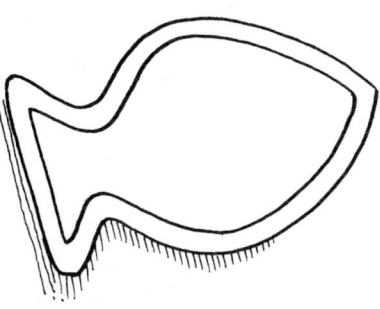

❸ Cut template along line B and place over each cut out shape and draw around it. Cut along this line and you will have 2 fish shapes from the one piece of card. (You will now have the required number of fish shapes.)

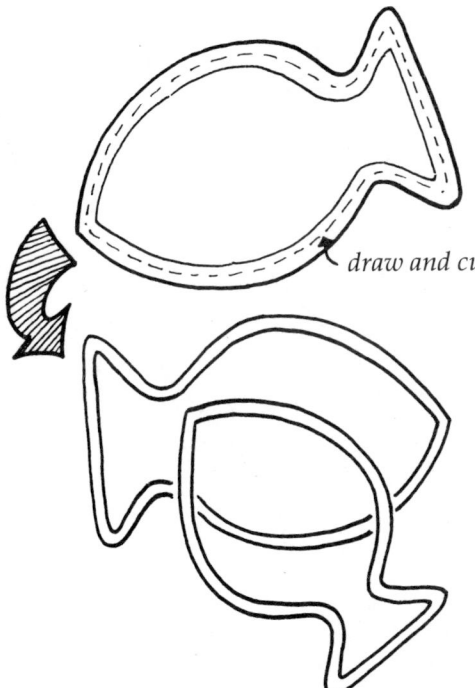
draw and cut

❹ Cut out backing for all the fish shapes in grease-proof paper using the templates.
❺ Cut out 10 or 15 circles of tissue paper per fish.

You will need
☆ black card: 1 A2 sheet makes 8 fish
☆ sheets of greaseproof paper
☆ circles 6-10cm in diameter cut from various brightly coloured sheets of tissue paper
☆ water-based glue (not PVA) and brushes or Pritt sticks
☆ pencils

Get the room ready
Put out for each child/parent:
- 1 black fish outline
- 1 greaseproof backing sheet (of the same size as the fish)
- 15 tissue paper circles in various colours

Put out on the table:
- water-based glue and brushes (or Pritt sticks)
- pencils
- a few extra tissue paper circles

What each child/parent does
❶ Take the greaseproof paper fish shape and glue on the tissue paper circles making sure that they overlap.

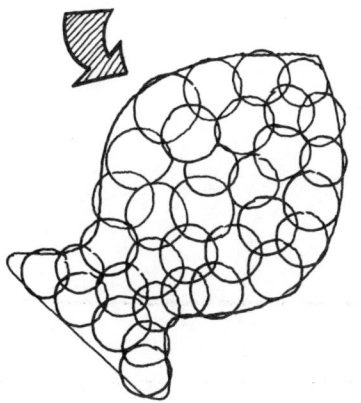

❷ Take the black fish outline and place over the greaseproof paper. Once it is in the right position, glue into place.

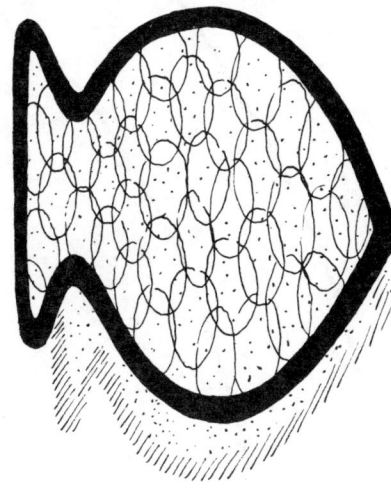

❸ Cut away any coloured circles hanging over the edge while the children are playing elsewhere, or leave it for them to do at home which saves having scissors around.
❹ If you hold the fish up to the light you get a stained glass effect. Suggest to the parents that they stick the fish to their window at home.

❺ Write on each child's name.

Activity Sheet – Catch of Fish

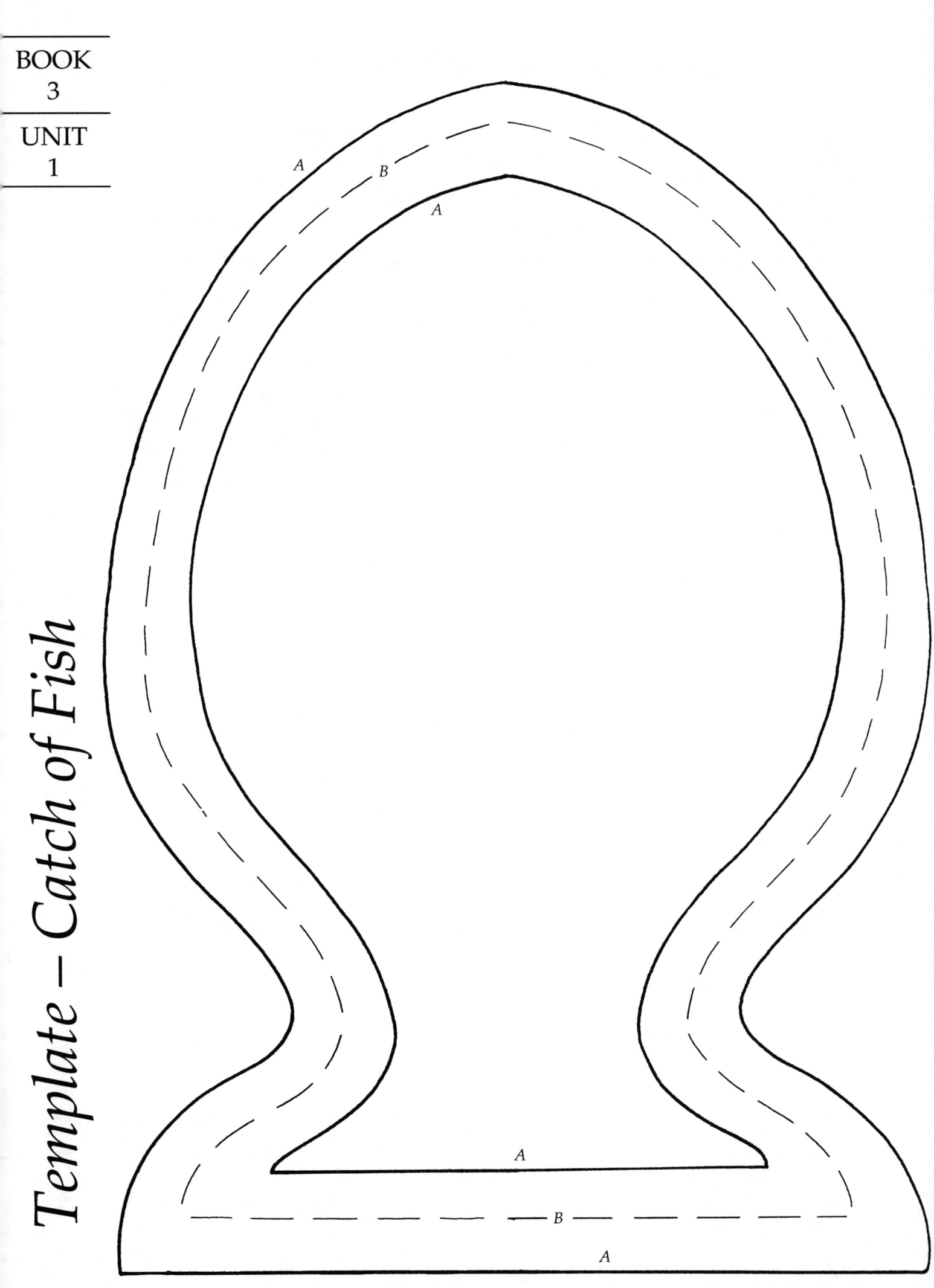

Jesus at the home of his friends

BOOK 3 UNIT 2

Jesus Helps Simon's Mother-in-law   *Mark 1:29-31*

This story comes very near the beginning of Mark's Gospel, but already Jesus is making a tremendous impression on people. Think about how you would feel if one of the members of your family were ill and you suddenly heard that you had visitors for dinner. Notice what Jesus does in verse 31 to heal Peter's mother-in-law. Look again at verse 31 and see her response to him.

Tell the story
Introduction:
Talk about hands and how we use them: for example to wave goodbye or to clap. Explain that some people who find it difficult to hear words, use their hands to speak, by using sign language. Teach the children and parents Makaton signs, such as "Hello","Mum","Dad", "Telephone" etc. and the signs that you will be using in the story. Make a game out of it.

Theme
To Jesus, everyone in the family matters.

Let's sing!
- " Everyone matters to Jesus "
- " You can weigh an elephant's auntie "
- " Jesus' hands are kind hands "

Activity
Make a family eating a meal together.

Visual aids
☆ Makaton signs (see separate sheet)

Story:
Tell the story very simply using the sign language, for example (the words with signs are in italic):
❶ Simon (*man*) and Andrew (*man*) arrived *home* from the synagogue (*church*) with *Jesus* for *dinner*.
❷ Elizabeth (*lady*) thought *"Help! dinner's* not ready and my *mother* is very *ill"*.
❸ Elizabeth (*lady*) told *Jesus* that her *mother* was in *bed* feeling very *ill*. *Jesus* took the *mother's* hand and *helped* her *sit up*.
❹ The *illness* went. She felt better (*healthy*).
❺ Elizabeth's *mother* gave *Jesus* a big smile and said *"Thank you"*. She got out of bed (*to stand*) and started laying the *table* and *helped* prepare the *dinner*.
❻ Soon the family were enjoying their *dinner*. Elizabeth's *mother* was very *happy*.

☞ *It is important for the storyteller to learn the signs so that they are confident in using them. Hopefully, the children will pick them up quickly and enjoy using them. You might want to select only some of the simpler signs, especially if you have a group with a large proportion of younger children.*

✎ Notes _____

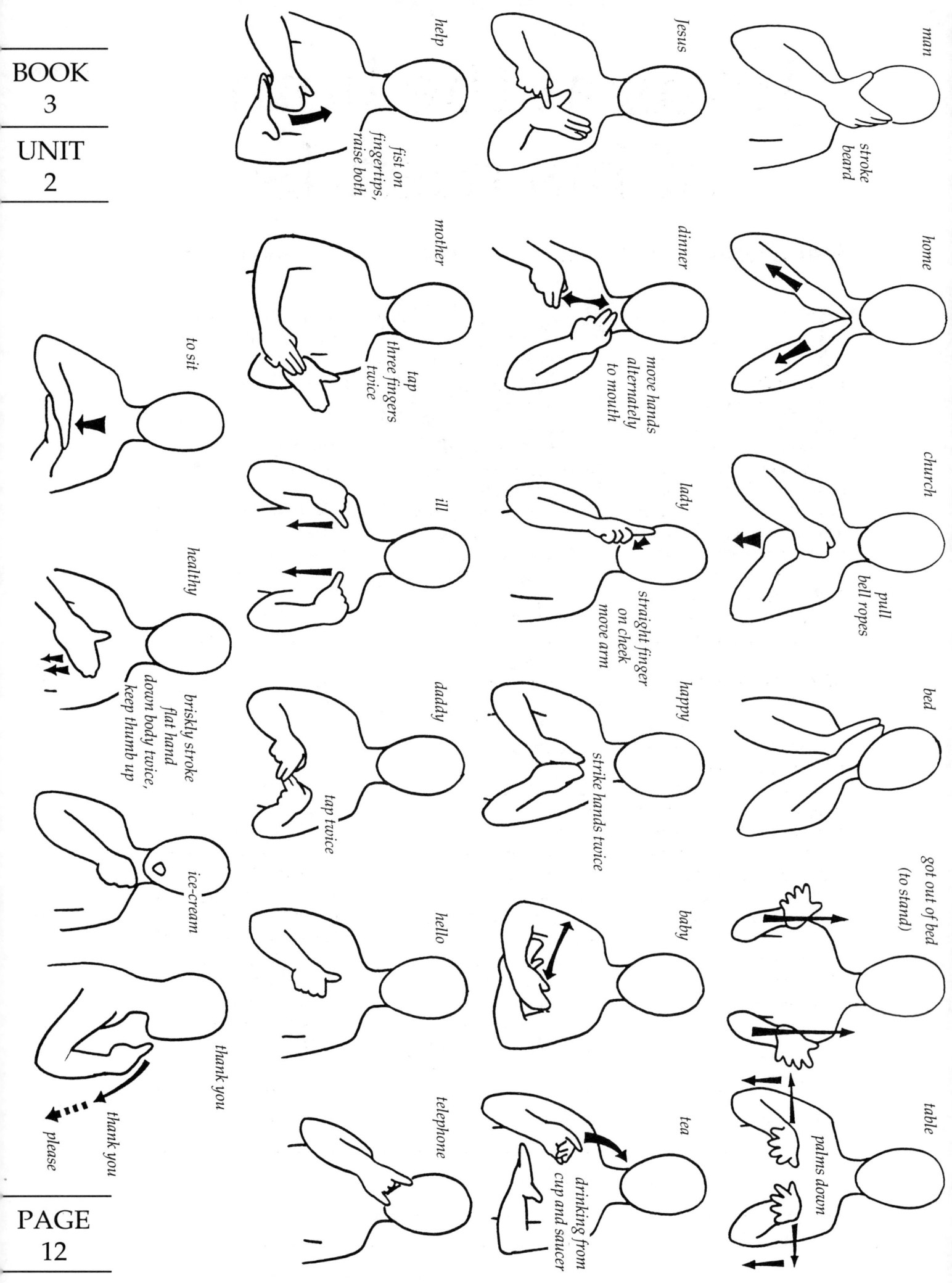

The family eating ice-cream

BOOK 3 UNIT 2

Prepare in advance
1. Cut out the template for family, table and chairs.
2. Once you have a cardboard template for the table, cut out as a whole without the centre fold.

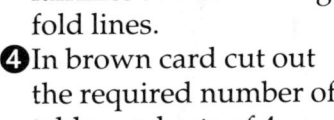

3. In white card cut out families and fold along fold lines.
4. In brown card cut out the required number of tables and sets of 4 chairs. Fold along the fold lines on the table.
5. Cut self adhesive sticky circles into strips of 4.

3. Stick onto the table cloth the 4 self adhesive circle plates.
4. Scrunch up the tissue and stick onto the plates for ice-cream.

5. Stick the table cloth and family onto the table top, and fold down the table legs.

You will need
- white card: 1 A2 sheet makes 4 familes
- thick brown card: 1 A2 sheet makes 4 sets of tables and chairs
- crayons
- 4 white or coloured large self adhesive circles per parent/child
- ice-cream coloured tissue paper (white, pink, etc)
- PVA glue and spreaders

Get the room ready
Put out for each child/parent:
- 1 family
- 1 table
- 4 chairs
- 1 strip of 4 circles

Put out on the table:
- tissue paper circles/squares
- crayons
- PVA glue and spreaders
- pencils

What each child/parent does
1. Colour in the faces, hair and bodies of the family.
2. Colour in the tablecloth if using white sticky circles for plates.

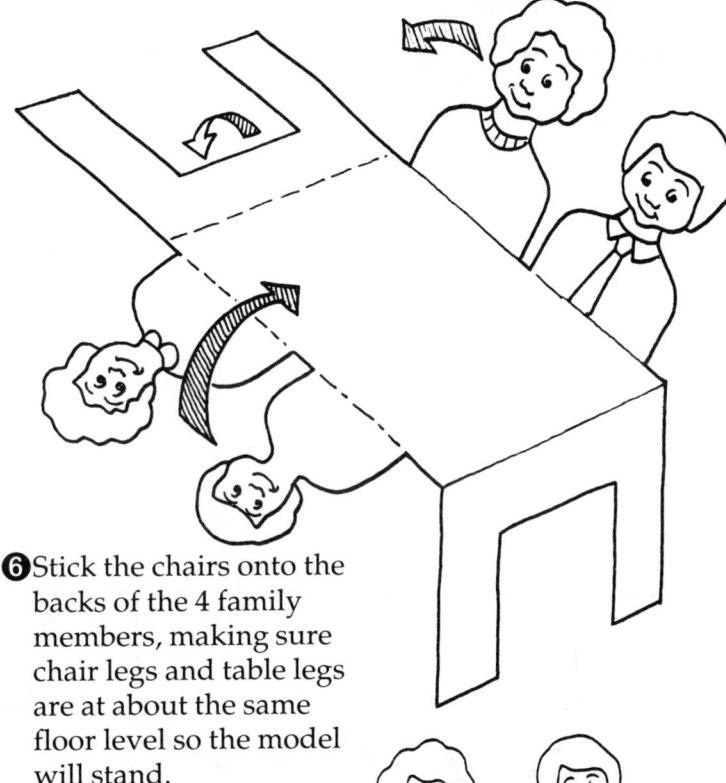

6. Stick the chairs onto the backs of the 4 family members, making sure chair legs and table legs are at about the same floor level so the model will stand.
7. Write on each child's name.

Activity Sheet – A Friend's Home

BOOK 3
UNIT 2

Template - A Friend's Home

family and tablecloth
cut one

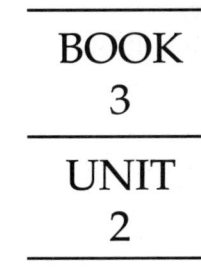

BOOK 3

UNIT 2

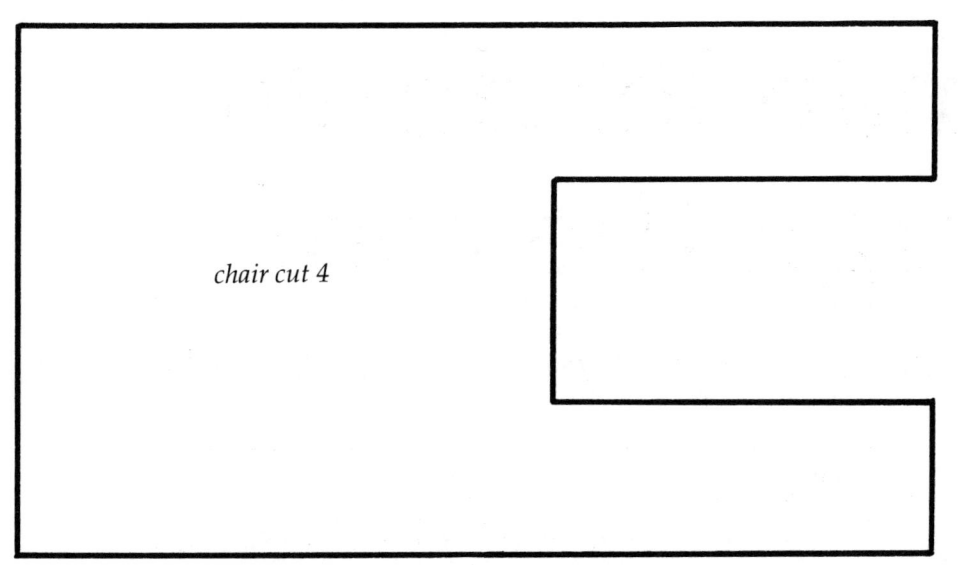

chair cut 4

place on fold (for cardboard template) *table cut one* *score line*

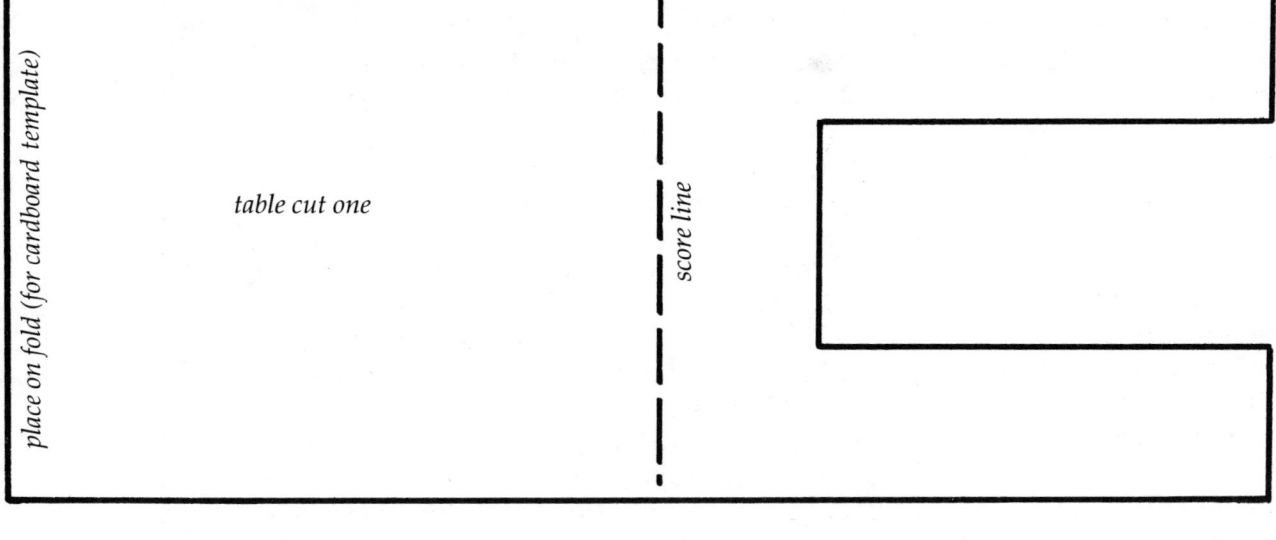

chair cut 4

Template – A Friend's Home

BOOK 3 UNIT 3

The man let down through the roof

Jesus Offers Forgiveness and Healing   Mark 2:1-12

How far would you go to help a friend? Notice in verse 4 the determination of the men and the lengths that they are prepared to go to to achieve their end. In verse 7 we read that the teachers of the law say that only God can forgive sins. What does this say to us about Jesus? What happens in verse 12 and what effect does this have on the crowd?

Tell the story

Introduction:
Show the children pictures of different sorts of houses. Look at the roofs. Explain that in Jesus' time in Palestine, the houses were white, flat roofed and the stairs were on the outside.

Story:

❶ This is a very straight-forward story, but very visual. Write it out in your own words, and give the man a name, eg Sam.

❷ Involve the children in the telling of the story by letting them act out the part of the friends.

❸ Mark in your story notes when the children are to move. You can actually incorporate this into your telling, eg "The friends picked up Sam on his bed (the children do it), and carried him to the house where Jesus was talking (they carry him across the room)".

❹ Some of the other children and mums could be the crowd all around the door of the house, so that Sam's friends can't get him in through the door.

❺ It is a good visual story, so have a lot of fun telling it. End with the main point that Jesus makes sick people better and helps them to say sorry.

Theme
Jesus is a special friend who forgives and heals.

Let's sing!
- " My God is so big "
- " God loves you and I love you "
- " I have hands that can clap, clap, clap "

Activity
Make a working model of a house with a hole in the roof and a man being lowered down.

Visual aids
- ☆ pictures of flats, semi-detached, terraced houses etc.
- ☆ a very large cardboard box to make into a house (see page 3) or a Wendy house, if you can give it a hole in the roof without damaging it
- ☆ a set of steps to put outside the box (stage steps would be ideal)
- ☆ a mat such as a bathmat
- ☆ a toddler puppet – to be the man
- ☆ children from the group to be the friends and Jesus himself

Helpful resources
- " The Lion Book of Stories of Jesus " (Section 11)
- " Lionel the Lame Man: The Wonderful Stories of Jesus " New Testament Book 1

The house with a hole in the roof

BOOK 3 — UNIT 3

Prepare in advance
❶ Cut out templates for steps, men, crowd and mat.
❷ Cut the card into rectangles 21cm by 29.7cm (A4 size), and measure 7cm from the long side. Fold over.

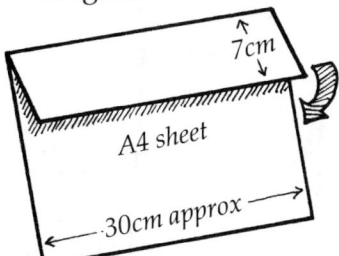

❸ Find the centre and fold in the 2 edges to meet the centre point.

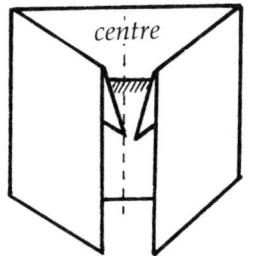

❹ Open the house out and make envelope folds in the corners of the roof. Secure the roof at the corners with staples or glue.
❺ Make a small hole in the roof about 3cm long.

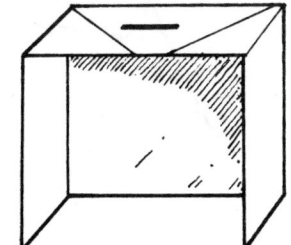

❻ Cut some white card into strips 13cm by 15cm. Draw around the step template to give 2 sets of steps.

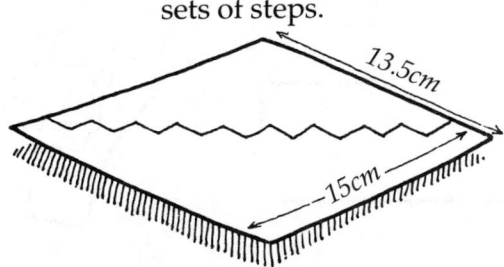

You will need
☆ white card for houses: 1 A2 sheet makes 4 houses
☆ white card for stairs: 1 A2 sheet makes 24 sets of stairs
☆ white card for people and mat
☆ crayons
☆ PVA glue and spreaders
☆ pencils
☆ paper clips
☆ stapler

❼ Using the template, cut out the mat from the white card.
❽ Using the template, cut out Jesus and the man from the white card.
❾ Using the template, cut out the crowd in white card, either as one group or cut out as 5 individuals to be coloured and stuck separately.
❿ Cut a piece of card 6cm by 2cm, and fold it in half.

Get the room ready
Put out for each child/parent:
- 1 house
- 1 set of steps
- 1 mat
- 1 Jesus
- 1 crowd
- 1 man
- 1 paper clip
- 1 folded piece of card

Put out on the table:
- PVA glue and spreaders
- crayons
- pencils

What each child/parent does
❶ Glue the steps onto the side of the house.

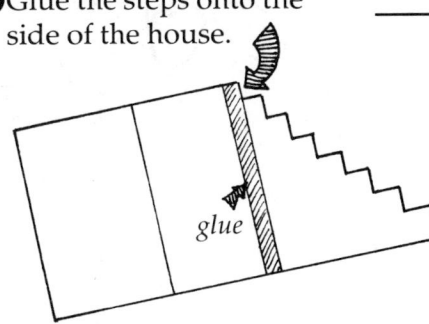

❷ Colour in Jesus, the man and the crowd (as a group or as individuals), then fold Jesus and the man down the centre which helps them to stand. Colour in the mat.
❸ Place the man on the mat and secure with the paper clip. Open up the house and push the flap of the mat through the hole in the roof and pull the man up onto the roof.
❹ Glue Jesus onto the folded piece of card and glue to the wall on the right-hand side inside the house.
❺ Stick the crowd onto the left-hand wall inside the house.
❻ Lower the man down into the room. After he has been made well, he can get off the mat and walk out through the door.

Activity Sheet – Through the Roof

Jesus at a wedding

Jesus Changes Water into Wine   John 2:1-11

BOOK 3
UNIT 4

Imagine what it would be like to go to a wedding where they ran out of food and drink! Why do you think that Jesus' mother tells him about the problem in verse 3? Look at verse 7 to see how the servants respond to Jesus' words. He must have spoken with an authority they recognised. Notice in verse 10 the reaction of the man in charge of the feast.

Tell the story
Introduction:
Talk about either a wedding using some of the appropriate wedding visual aids or play a party game – eg pass the parcel (not too many layers) and ask the children if they enjoy parties. Ask what they eat and drink at parties. This leads into talking about Jesus being invited to a wedding party and how he, too, enjoyed himself.

Story:
After the introduction pick up the story with Jesus at the party using the puppets and the yoghurt pots for water jugs. Show the children what a real water pot might have looked like if you have one yourself.

❶ Mary tells Jesus that the wine has run out.
❷ The servants are told to fill the pots with water.
❸ The servant takes a jug of water to the man in charge.
❹ The water has turned to wine.

☞ *Your main points should be that Jesus enjoys being with people (introduction) and he helps them (main story).*

Theme
Jesus enjoys being with people and helps them.

Let's Sing!
- " God knows me and you "
- " Jesus' love is very wonderful "
- " God is good "

Activity
Make 3-D water pot cards.

Visual aids
☆ wedding invitation
☆ wedding photograph
☆ mum in a wedding dress
☆ a child dressed as bridesmaid or pageboy
☆ glove puppets: Jesus, Jesus' mother, a servant
☆ pot, such as a small yoghurt pot, for servant to carry
☆ 6 large yoghurt pots
☆ a large earthenware pot or jug if you have one

Helpful resources
- " Jesus Goes to a Wedding: The Wonderful Stories of Jesus " New Testament Book 1
- " The Lion Book of Stories of Jesus " (Section 9)

✎ Notes _____
_____
_____
_____
_____
_____

BOOK 3 UNIT 4

Activity Sheet – Wedding at Cana

3-D water pot card

Prepare in advance
1. Cut out template for pot card, the two sizes of pot, the servant and Jesus.
2. Cut the orange/brown card into rectangles 21cm by 15cm and fold in half to give 10.5cm by 15cm.
3. Place the pot card template on the card making sure the straight side of the pot is along the fold.
4. Draw round and cut out the cards, making sure you don't cut the fold where the pot touches it.

You will need
- ☆ orange/brown coloured card: 1 A4 sheet makes 2 pots
- ☆ strips of orange/brown card
- ☆ scraps of orange/brown card for small pots (preferably a different shade from the main card)
- ☆ white card: 1 A4 sheet makes 4 sets of figures
- ☆ PVA glue and spreaders
- ☆ coloured crayons
- ☆ pencils

5. Inside the pot card mark on shaded areas A and B.
6. In the main orange/brown card cut out strips of card 15cm by 2cm and 6cm by 2cm. You will need one of each per pot. Mark the strips as shown in the template and fold along the lines.

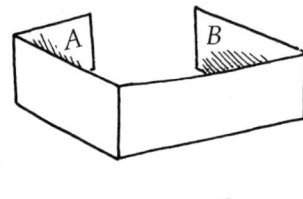

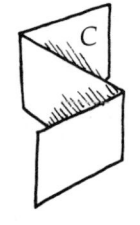

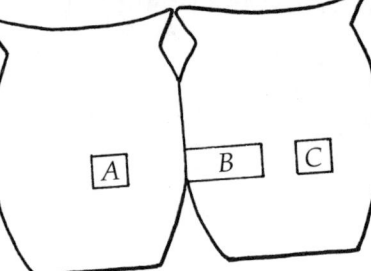

7. Stick A and B onto the parts shaded A and B on the pot cards.
8. Stick C into position about 1cm away from B.

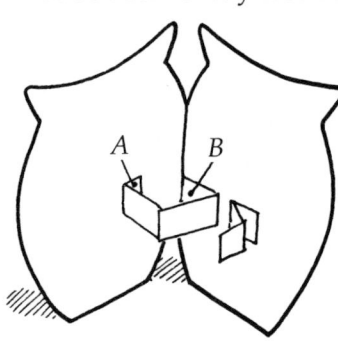

9. Cut out both sizes of small pot from the scraps of card. You need one small pot and 2 of the slightly larger ones.

10. In white card cut out the required number of figures, one Jesus and one servant per card, per child.

Get the room ready
Put out for each child/parent:
- 1 pot card
- 2 pots
- 1 small pot
- 1 set of figures

Put out on the table:
- crayons
- PVA glue and spreaders
- pencils

What each child/parent does
1. Crayon in Jesus and servant, making sure they are facing each other with Jesus on the right.
2. Stick the smallest pot into the slit under the arm of the servant.
3. Stick the figures into position on the card, the servant with the pot and the 2 larger pots onto the strip that folds out, and Jesus onto strip C.
4. Write each child's name on the card.

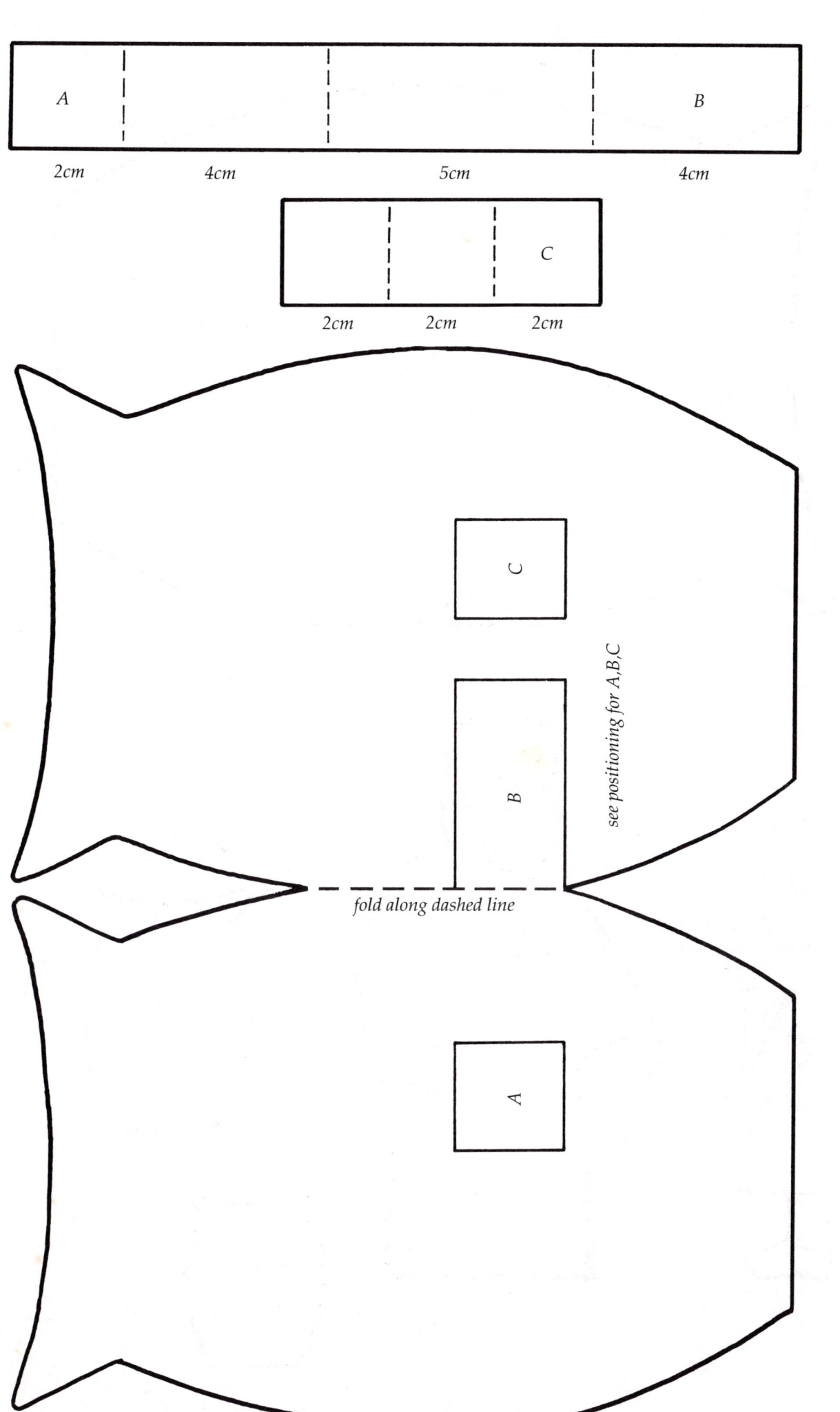

Template – Wedding at Cana

BOOK 3 UNIT 4

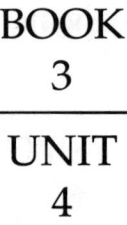

BOOK 3
UNIT 4

Template – Wedding at Cana

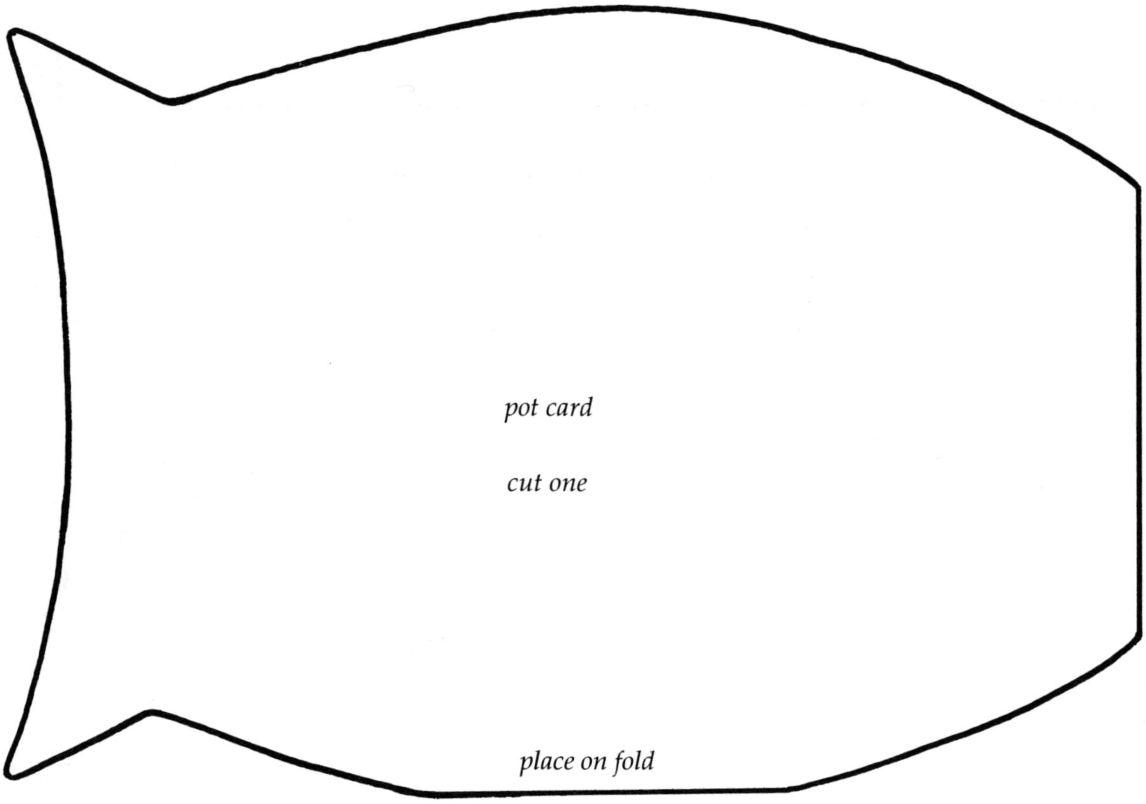

pot card

cut one

place on fold

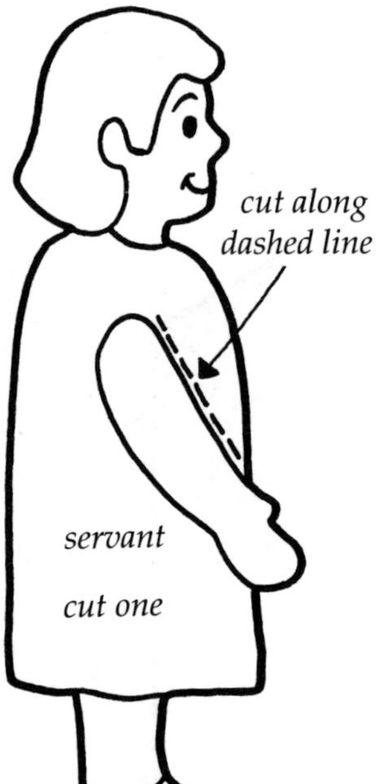

cut along dashed line

servant
cut one

Jesus
cut one

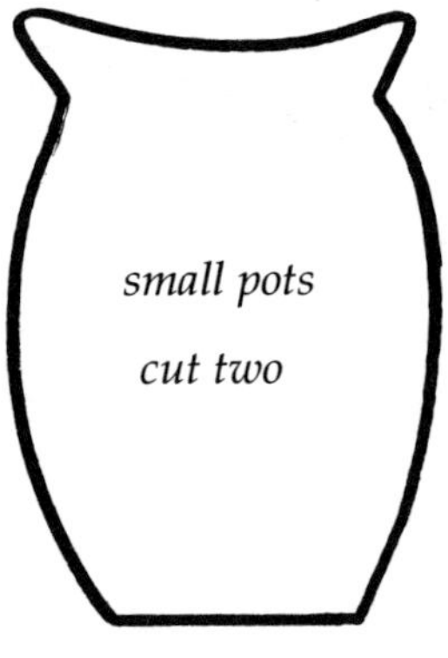

small pots
cut two

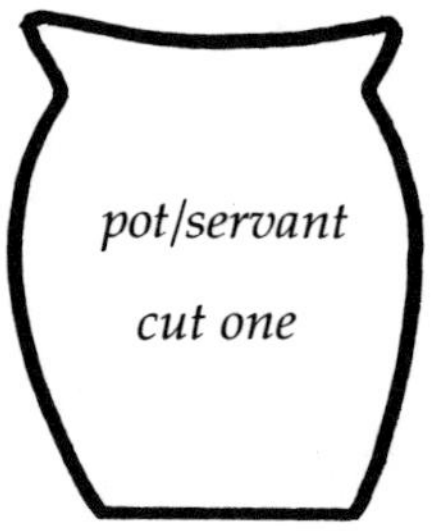

pot/servant
cut one

Matthew's special guest

BOOK 3
UNIT 5

Jesus Asks a Tax Collector to Follow Him

Matthew 9:9-13

Are you an impulsive person? Do you do things suddenly? Here Matthew seems to act impulsively but his impulse is a response to the tremendous authority of Jesus. What does verse 10 tell us about the people Jesus eats with? See in verse 11 how the religious authorities feel about this. Notice that they don't actually challenge Jesus though. Who do they direct their questions at and how does Jesus hear? Look at verses 11 and 12 to see why they do this.

Tell the story

This story needs 2 people, a narrator and someone to act out the part of Matthew. Read the story in the Bible and *The Lion Book of Bible Stories and Prayers* and then write it out in your own words. Make a note of the times when Matthew will need a little extra time to act out the part, eg when laying the table.

Introduction:
Introduce Matthew. He has a big house and lots of money, but he isn't very happy. People don't like him.

Story:
❶ One day Matthew is sitting in his office counting his money.
❷ Jesus sees him at work, and asks him to follow him.
❸ Matthew responds.
❹ He decides to throw a party for Jesus. He invites his friends and gets things ready.
❺ Matthew's guests arrive. Invite the mums and children to play Simon Says, or something similar that can be kept quick and fairly simple).
❻ Matthew claps his hands for quiet (everybody settles down again) and he invites his guests to listen to Jesus. He has decided to follow him, and he wants to tell everybody about him.

Theme
Jesus is a friend to share with others.

Let's sing!
- " Come into his presence "
- " God loves you and I love you "
- " Who's the King of the jungle? "

Activity
Make biscuits with happy faces.

Visual aids
☆ large table
☆ chair(s)
☆ money and money bags
☆ a large account book
☆ invitation cards, tablecloth, some party food

Helpful resources
- " The Lion Book of Bible Stories and Prayers " (Section 24)

✎ Notes _____
_____
_____
_____
_____

BOOK 3 UNIT 5

Activity Sheet – Matthew's Guest

Biscuits with happy faces

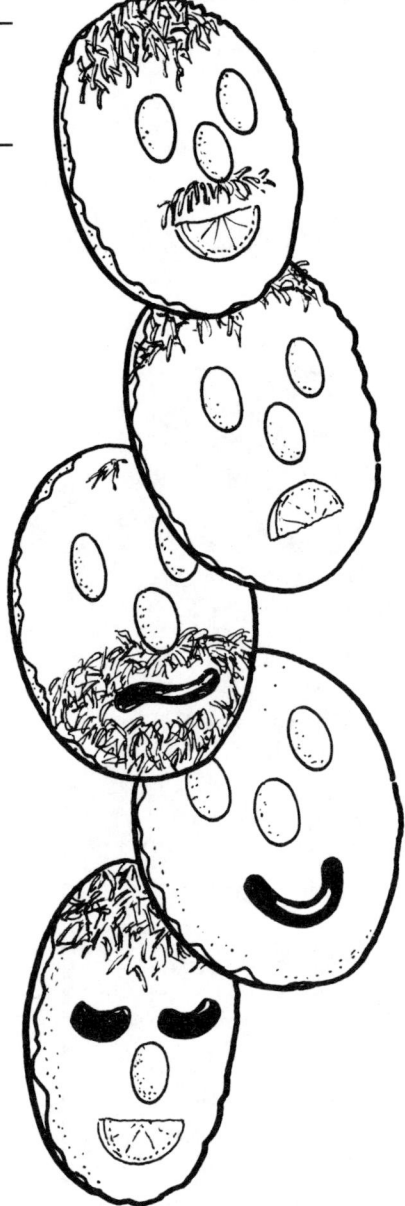

> **You will need**
> ☆ 1 plain round biscuit per parent/child
> ☆ some roll-out fondant icing: a 250 gm packet makes about 15 biscuits
> ☆ smarties for eyes and noses
> ☆ orange sugar halves for mouth or little pieces of red liquorice
> ☆ vermicelli for hair
> ☆ margarine tubs to hold the sweets and vermicelli
> ☆ greaseproof paper, roll or sheets
> ☆ pastry brushes (ask the team to bring the week before)

Get the room ready

Make sure the tables are clean, or covered with PVC tablecloths.
Put out for each child/parent:
- 1 rectangle of greaseproof to hold:
- 1 biscuit
- 1 circle of icing
- 3 smarties
- 1 orange sugar segment or liquorice

Put out on the table:
- pastry brushes
- margarine tub with a little water
- margarine tub with vermicelli
- pencils

Prepare in advance

❶ Cut some greaseproof paper into 12cm squares.
❷ Cut some more greaseproof paper into rectangles 20cm by 15cm.
❸ On the morning of the session roll out the icing at home and cut with a circular pastry cutter to fit onto the biscuits.
❹ Put icing circles on greaseproof squares and put them into a plastic container with a lid to keep them pliable.

What each child/parent does

❶ Moisten biscuit with water.
❷ Stick on the icing.

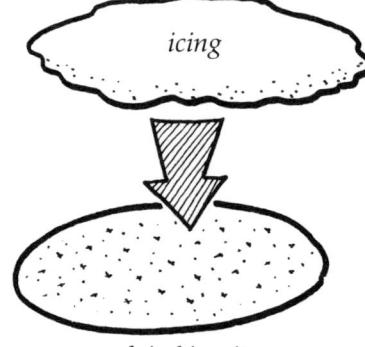

❸ Stick on smarties for eyes and nose and orange segment for a mouth.
❹ Slightly moisten the top of the biscuit.
❺ Shake on vermicelli for hair.

❻ Write each child's name on a rectangular piece of greaseproof and use it to wrap up the biscuit to take it home.

☞ Get them all to take their biscuits home rather than letting them eat them straight away. This should stop arguments and upsets if some are allowed to eat now and others aren't. You may wish to use the happy/sad face badge activity from Book 2, Unit 6 instead.

Why Zacchaeus climbed a tree

BOOK 3 UNIT 6

Jesus Welcomes Zacchaeus *Luke 19:1-10*

We often notice change by seeing the difference before and after. Make a list of all of the things we find out about Zacchaeus in verses 1-4. See how Zacchaeus responds to what Jesus says in verse 5. Meeting Jesus causes a dramatic change in Zacchaeus' life. What does verse 8 tell us about how he shows this?

Theme
Jesus changes people's lives.

Let's sing!
- "Jesus' love is a powerful love"
- "God is for me"
- "Who's that sitting in a sycamore tree?"
- "Zacchaeus was a very little man"

Activity
Make a little man up a tree.

Visual aids
☆ a large cardboard cut-out tree (see page 3)
☆ a number of the children to be a crowd
☆ a child to be Zacchaeus
☆ clothes for Zacchaeus: an adult's t-shirt (in a rich colour), a hat, a length of material for a belt
☆ a child to be Jesus, wearing a plain white adult's t-shirt
☆ a table and 2 chairs, 2 cups and saucers to represent Zacchaeus' house

Helpful resources
"The Man in the Tree: The Wonderful Stories of Jesus" New Testament Book 1

Tell the story
Introduction:
Play a "spot the difference" game. Have 4 sets of objects, which are the same except for one obvious difference: a cake with 1 candle/a cake with 3 candles; a pair of red wellies/a pair of yellow wellies; a large spoon/a small spoon; a red drinking beaker with one handle/a red drinking beaker with 2 handles.

Involve the children and parents in spotting the differences between the objects.

Explain that today's story is about some big differences in one person's life after he met Jesus.

Story:
❶ Have the tree in position.
❷ Set the scene by explaining how crowds of people were lining the street because they had heard that Jesus was in town. (Get your crowd to stand to the side of the tree, not in front.)
❸ Introduce the unpopular Zacchaeus.
❹ Zacchaeus joins the crowd but he can't see, (have him jumping up to see) and no one will let him through. He sees the tree and climbs it.
❺ Jesus stops under the tree and tells Zacchaeus to come down.
❻ Jesus goes to Zacchaeus' house and has tea with him.
❼ Zacchaeus promises to change – meeting Jesus has had a great effect on him.

☞ *As you tell the story very simply, use Zacchaeus, Jesus and the crowd. Try to use words that point out the movement so that they can follow, eg "Jesus said to Zacchaeus, 'Let's go over to your house for tea.'"*

BOOK 3 UNIT 6

A little man up a tree

Prepare in advance

❶ Cut out the Zacchaeus template in cereal packet card.
❷ Cut the white card into rectangles 11cm by 12cm.
❸ Fold the white card in half (11cm by 6cm) and draw around the Zacchaeus template, making sure the straight edge of the template is placed on the fold of the card. Cut out.

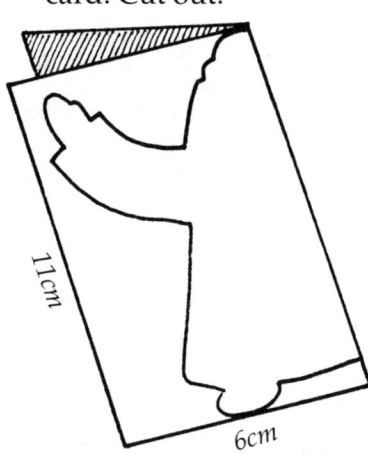

❹ Fold each A3 sheet of green sugar paper into 4 (halve it then halve it again).

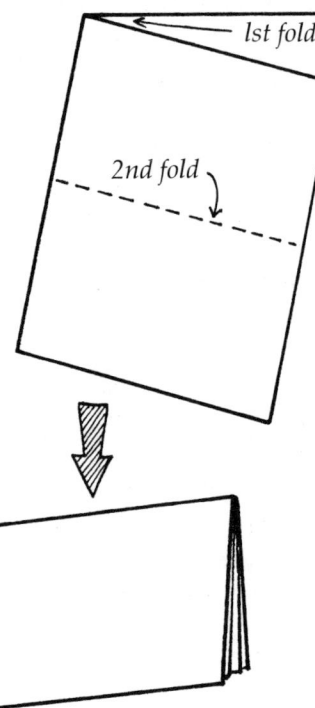

You will need
☆ green sugar paper: 1 A3 sheet makes 4 sets of leaves
☆ empty kitchen towel rolls (toilet rolls are too short)
☆ white card: 1 A2 sheet makes 15 Zacchaeus
☆ PVA glue and spreaders
☆ crayons and pencils

❺ Cut out the leaf template in cereal packet card.
❻ Place the leaf template on folded green paper. Draw around and cut out.

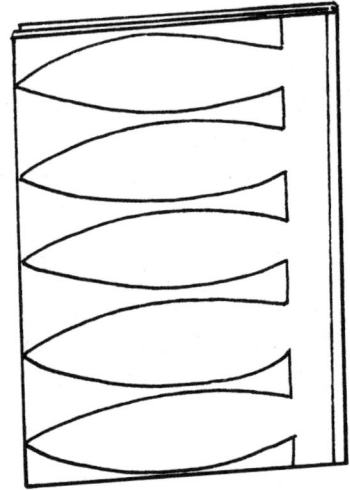

Get the room ready
Put out for each child/parent:
- 1 tube
- 1 set of leaves
- 1 Zacchaeus

Put out on the table:
- PVA glue and spreaders
- crayons
- pencils

What each child/parent does
❶ Colour in Zacchaeus front and back.
❷ Put glue on the straight top edge of the leaves.

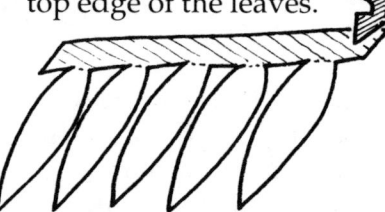

glue here

❸ Stick the top edge of the leaves inside the tube, and fold the leaf parts out and down.

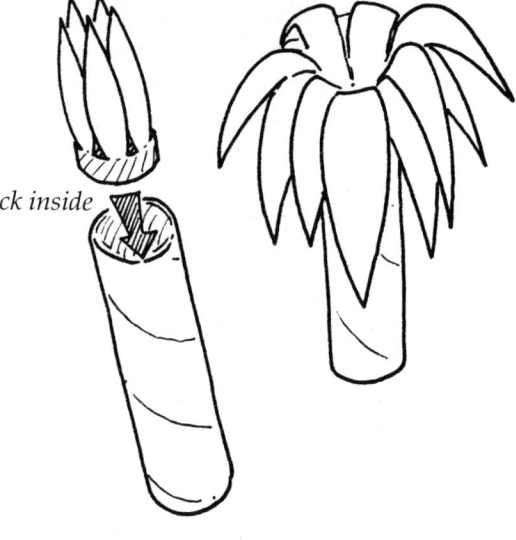

stick inside

❹ Put a little glue on one hand and one foot (same side of body) of Zacchaeus, and stick him on, climbing up the tree.

❺ Write on each child's name.

Activity Sheet – Zacchaeus

Only one said thank you

BOOK 3 UNIT 7

Jesus Heals Ten Lepers *Luke 17:11-19*

Think for a moment about how much we take for granted. Are we always as grateful as we should be? Here is a story about ten people, nine of whom don't bother to say thank you. Where does verse 11 tell us this story takes place? What does Jesus ask the lepers to do in verse 14? In verse 16 we read that only one came back to say thank you to Jesus. What question does Jesus ask him?

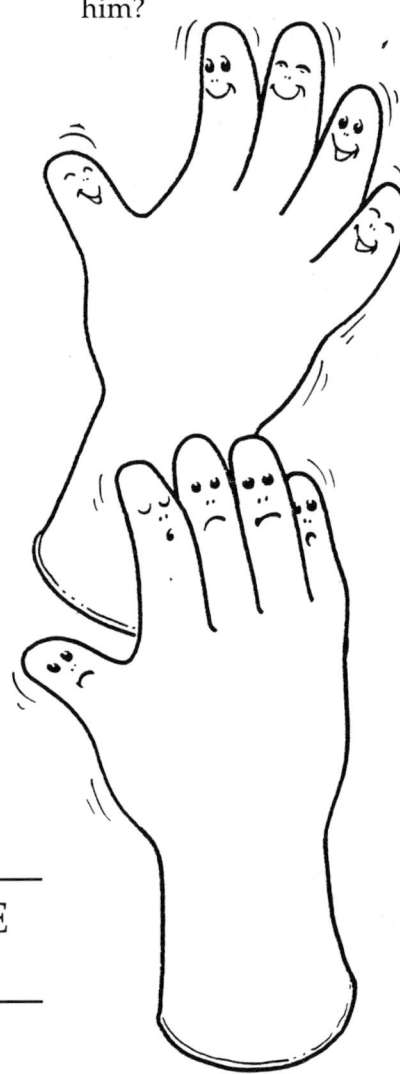

Theme
Jesus shows God's love and reminds us to be thankful.

Let's sing!
" You can weigh an elephant's auntie "
" God's love is like a circle "
" Lord we come to worship you "

Activity
Make a hand puppet and a finger puppet.

Visual aids
☆ a pair of rubber gloves with happy faces drawn on one side of the fingers and sad faces on the other
☆ a little paper hat for the man who went back to say thank you

Helpful resources
" The Lion Book of Bible Stories and Prayers " (section 29)
" Barty says Thank You: The Wonderful Stories of Jesus " New Testament Book 1
" Round and Round the Garden "

Tell the story

Introduction:
Sing a finger rhyme (with the actions) involving ten fingers, such as "I've got ten little fingers and they all belong to me" from "Round and Round the Garden".

Story:
❶ Tell the story about ten lepers who were very sad because they had an illness which... Show the sad side of the gloves as you tell the story.
❷ So, Jesus healed them all. Turn the gloves round to show the happy faces.
❸ But only one went back to Jesus to say thank you. Now hold up one finger.
❹ After he spoke to Jesus... Put hat on one finger to show that this man was different.
❺ Continue by thinking briefly about things we need to say thank you for.

PAGE 28

Glove and finger puppet

BOOK 3 UNIT 7

Prepare in advance
Glove puppet:
1. Cut out template for glove, body, face, hair and beard in cereal packet card.
2. Cut the green card into A4 rectangle size and fold in half to make 21cm by 15cm.
3. Place glove template onto card, draw round and cut out gloves.
4. Make a crease along the dotted lines.
5. Using a stapler, staple the sides of the glove together. The creases make it easier for a child's hand to slip into the glove.

6. Cut white self adhesive circles into strips of 9 circles.

Finger puppet:
1. Cut brightly coloured felt into rectangles 4cm by 14cm.
2. Fold the rectangles in half, 4cm by 7cm.
3. Using the body template cut out 2 pieces for the man front and back.
4. Using a sewing machine, sew the front and back together making sure to leave the gap at the bottom.

You will need
- old cereal packets
- green card: 1 A4 sheet makes 1 glove
- 9 white self adhesive circles per glove
- stapler
- flesh coloured felt for face
- brightly coloured felt for body
- brown/black coloured felt for hair
- scraps of blue and red coloured felt for features
- PVA glue and spreaders
- crayons
- pencils
- sewing machine

5. Using the face, beard and hair templates as a guide, cut out face in flesh coloured felt and beard/hair in brown/black felt.
6. Cut out eyes and mouths in the scraps of felt and place in margarine tubs.

Get the room ready
Put out for each child/parent:
- a green glove
- a strip of circles
- a felt body
- a face
- beard and hair

Put out on the table:
- PVA glue and spreaders
- crayons
- pencils
- margarine tubs containing eyes and mouths

What each child/parent does
1. Draw faces onto the 9 circles and stick them onto the gloves keeping clear of the thumb.

2. On the felt body stick on face, beard with hair, eyes and mouths.
3. Put the finger puppet onto the thumb of the glove.

☞ As the children re-enact the story they take the finger puppet off the glove and put it on a finger on the other hand. Only one person went back to say "Thank you"!

Activity Sheet – Saying Thank You

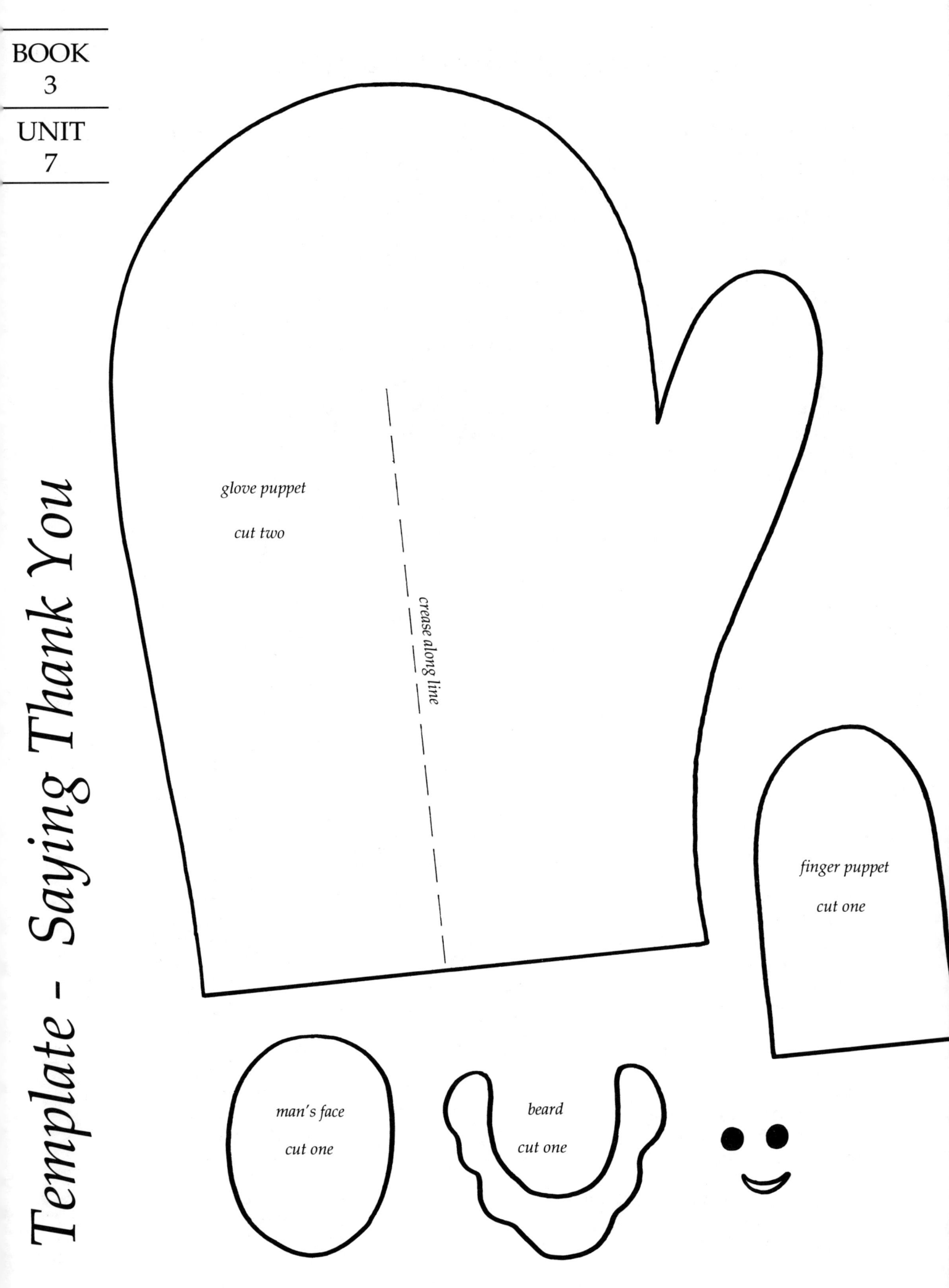

Meeting Jesus

Jesus Restores Bartimaeus' Sight Mark 10:46-52

BOOK 3
UNIT 8

Have you ever wanted something so much that you've let nothing stand in your way? In this story Bartimaeus is going to let no one stop him from speaking to Jesus. What is the reaction of the crowd in verse 48? See how in verse 51 Bartimaeus knows just what he wants and is confident that Jesus can fulfil this need.

Tell the story
Introduction:
Start by playing some games to communicate the idea that when you can't see, you depend more on touch and sound.

Get a child to put his/her hand into a pillow slip to guess what is hidden inside it.

Hand out simple musical instruments if your group has them – including to the babies. The leader will need one of each instrument. The leader hides behind a board or sheet so that the children cannot see which instrument is being played. But if the children have the same instrument, they play theirs as well. Or you could mime playing an instrument and the children mime along. Put the instruments away at the end of the activity.

Story:
❶ Explain that today's story is about a man who could not see things, but he could hear and touch. He couldn't see a drum, but he could hear it. He could hear a quiet whisper, and he could tell if there was only one person walking, or if there was a large crowd – just by listening.

❷ Today a large crowd of people were rushing by, and he wanted to know what was going on. So he had to shout out, "What is going on?" People shouted back, "Jesus is walking past!" And so he shouted again, "I want to see Jesus!"

❸ Everybody going by told him to be quiet. Jesus, though, stopped, and he told Blind Bartimaeus to come to him, and he asked him what he wanted. Bartimaeus said that he wanted to be able to see. Jesus answered him, "Trust in me, you can see."

❹ Bartimaeus found himself looking into Jesus' face. He danced down the road, very happy, following Jesus.

Theme
Jesus never ignores us.

Let's sing!
" Everyone matters to Jesus "
" Lord you gave me joy in my heart "
" I have hands "

Activity
Make a magic picture.

Visual aids
☆ toddler puppet dressed as Bartimaeus – a plain adult t-shirt with a scrap of material for a sash
☆ headdress – same method as for activity
☆ a bowl for begging
☆ household objects such as a sponge, orange, toy telephone etc.
☆ several pillow cases, 1 per object
☆ musical instruments such as a drum, bells, tambourine etc.
☆ board/sheet/box to hide instruments behind

Helpful resources
" The Lion Book of Bible Stories and Prayers " (Section 26)
" The Lion Book of Stories of Jesus " (Section 32)

A magic picture

BOOK 3 / UNIT 8

Activity Sheet – Meeting Jesus

Prepare in advance
1. Cut coloured card into rectangles 26cm by 12cm.
2. Mark each rectangle as in the diagram and fold along the lines.

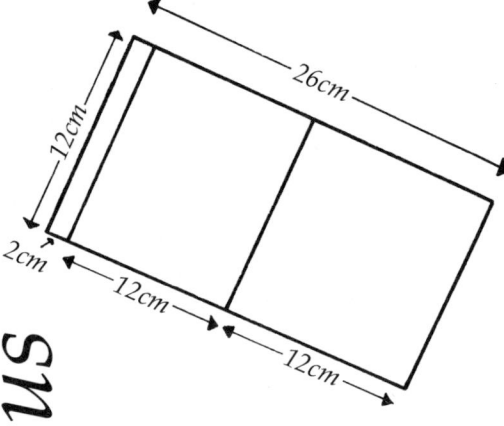

3. Cut out the picture frame template in cereal packet card.
4. Place the template in position, draw around it and cut out middle and the thumb holes.

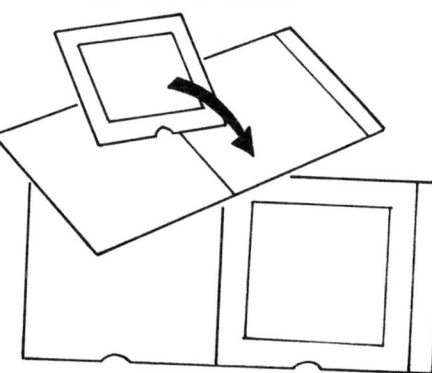

5. Cut the white card into rectangles 12cm by 10cm and 12cm by 9.5cm, one of each per picture.
6. Cut out the thumb hole in the 12cm by 10cm rectangle.

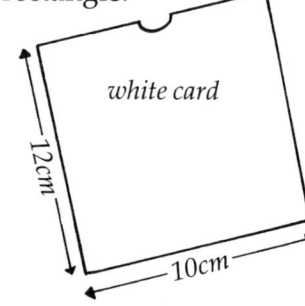

white card

7. Cut the OHP acetates into rectangles 12cm by 11cm.
8. Take the smaller white rectangle (12cm by 9.5cm) and draw a line 1.5cm in on the long side. Glue just above this line and stick on the acetate. Some acetate will hang over at the bottom - don't cut this off.

a little acetate will overlap white card

You will need
- old cereal packets
- OHP acetate sheets: 1 A4 sheet makes 4 pictures
- white card: 1 A2 sheet makes 9 pictures
- brightly coloured card: 1 A2 sheet makes 6 picture frames
- black OHP water based pens (not permanent)
- crayons
- pencils
- PVA glue and spreaders

Get the room ready
Put out for each child/parent:
- 1 coloured picture frame
- 1 white rectangle with thumb hole
- 1 glued OHP acetate and card

Put out on the table:
- black OHP pens
- crayons
- PVA glue and spreaders
- pencils

What each child/parent does
1. Take the coloured picture frame and glue along the 2cm edge and stick on the white rectangle, making sure the thumb holes are all on the same edge.

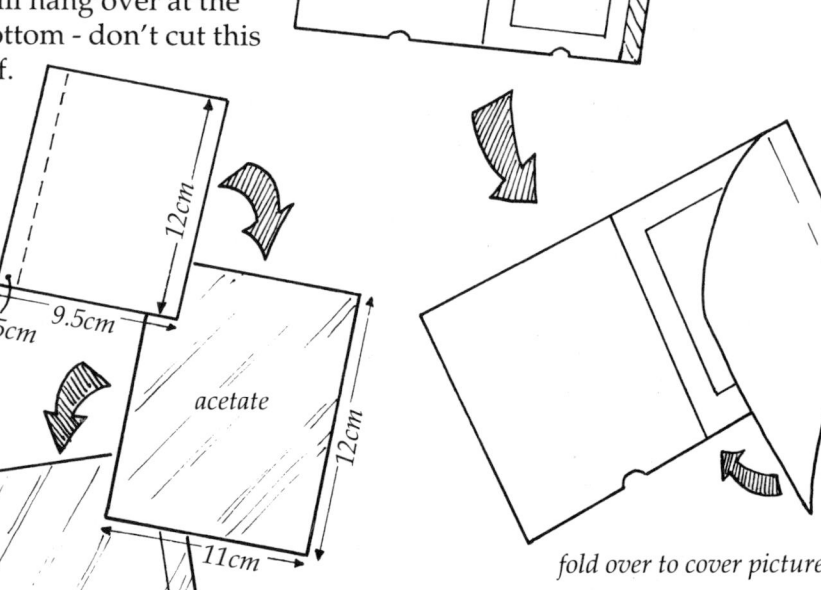

fold over to cover picture frame

2. Fold the white rectangle in to cover the picture frame hole.

BOOK 3 UNIT 9

The little girl who got better

Jesus Heals an Official's Daughter

Matthew 9:18-19, 23-26

Why do you think that the official goes to Jesus? In verse 19 we read that Jesus responds immediately to the man's request. How do people respond to Jesus in verse 23? See how advanced preparations are in the same verse. What does Jesus do in verse 25? Is this different from, say, the healing of the man at the pool? (Unit 10) Are you surprised at verse 26?

Theme
Jesus cares for us when we are poorly.

Let's sing!
" My God is so big "
" Jesus, Jesus, here I am "
" Lord you gave me joy in my heart "

Activity
Make a girl in bed who gets better.

Visual aids
☆ glove puppets: little girl, father, mother, Jesus and servant
☆ a shoe box for a bed or a small doll's cot with sheet/blanket

Helpful resources
" Becky Gets Better: The Wonderful Stories of Jesus " New Testament Book 1

Tell the story
Introduction:
Start with a game such as "Ring a ring of roses" or a short version of "Farmer's in his den". If the group has more babies and under 2s, then get them to play "Round and round the garden" sitting on their parents' knees.

Story:
❶ Introduce the little girl puppet. "This is Jenny. She is a happy little girl and likes playing games... but... she is feeling poorly."
❷ Continue the story with the aid of the puppets.

☞ *To involve the children more in the telling of the story you could give out glove puppets and instruments to the children to be the official mourners at the house, and use them accordingly.*

✎ *Notes* _____
_____
_____
_____
_____
_____
_____

Girl in bed/girl well

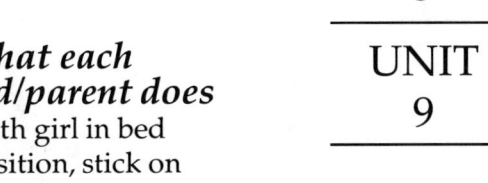

BOOK 3

UNIT 9

Prepare in advance
1. Make a card template of girl A, and girl B in bed, and dress, coat, hair, bedding.
2. In pink card draw and cut out girl A and girl B.
3. Fold the girl in bed B along the dotted line.
4. Stick onto the girl A placing the fold of B against the line of dashes on the girl. Make sure the feet are on the top so that when you fold up the bedclothes the feet become the face.

You will need
- pink card: 1 A4 sheet makes 2 girls
- coloured sugar paper for dress, coat, hair
- wall paper/wrapping paper for bedding
- PVA glue and spreaders
- pencils
- black crayons

Get the room ready
Put out for each child/parent:
- 1 girl
- 1 set bedclothes
- 1 hair
- 1 dress
- 1 coat

Put out on the table:
- PVA glue and spreaders
- black crayons
- pencils

What each child/parent does
1. With girl in bed position, stick on bedclothes.
2. Draw on sad, ill face.

bed position

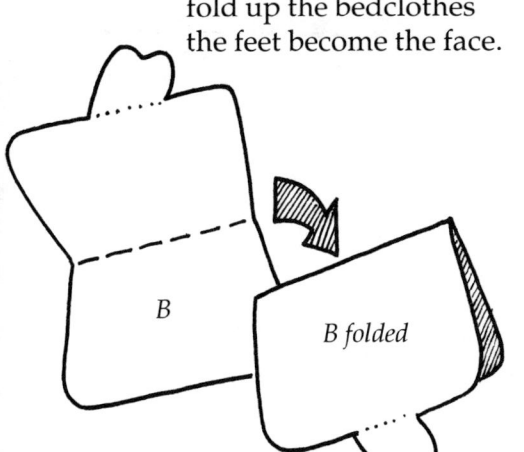

B folded — *stick fold along dashed line* — *well position*

3. With girl in well position, stick on hair, dress and coat.
4. Draw on happy face and feet.

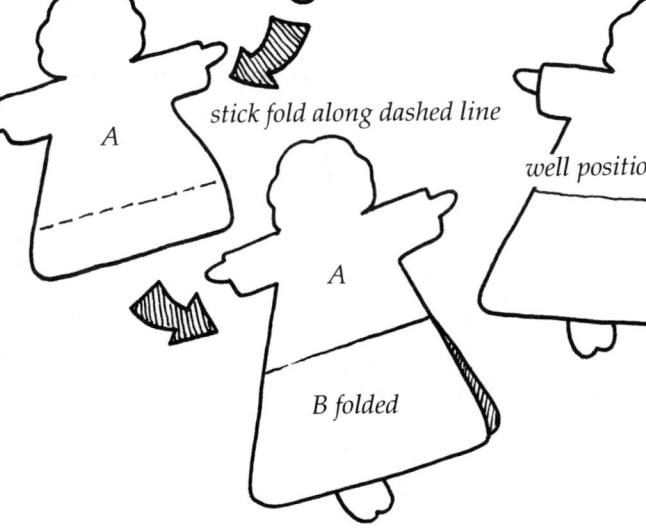

5. Cut out the bedclothes in wallpaper or wrapping paper.
6. Cut out dress, coat and hair in sugar paper of appropriate colours.

Activity Sheet – The Little Girl

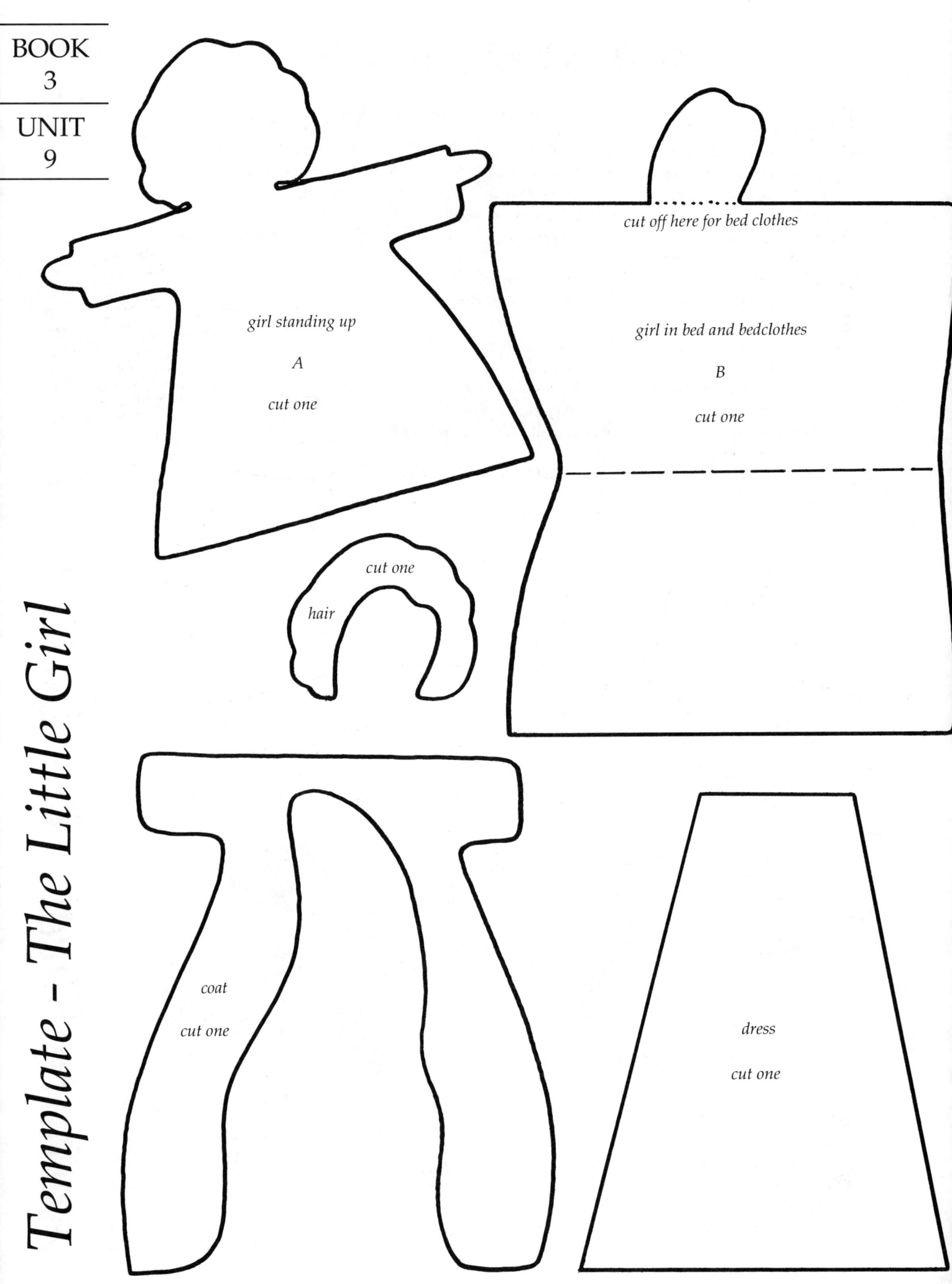

The man beside the pool

BOOK 3

UNIT 10

Jesus Brings Healing to a Crippled Man John 5:1-9,14

If you were ill, would you want to get better? Look at verse 7 for the answer that the man gives to Jesus. How long does verse 5 tell us the man had been ill? Jesus heals in many different ways. Here he heals with a word and according to verse 13 the man doesn't even seem to know who Jesus is.

Tell the story

Introduction:
Ask the children if any of them have a paddling pool at home. Find out if any of them go to the swimming baths, and if any of them have been to an open air swimming pool. Explain that today's story happened at a pool just outside the city of Jerusalem, which was like an open air swimming pool, measuring 60m by 100m.

Theme
Jesus heals.

Let's sing!
- " Jesus' love is very wonderful "
- " Have you seen the pussy cat? "
- " Jesus, Jesus here I am "

Activity
Make a man who walks and runs.

Visual aids
☆ the lid from a sandpit or a baby bath
☆ a small amount of water in the above
☆ 10-15 Duplo men

Story:

❶ Using the Duplo men, introduce the crowds of sick people lying around the pool with their families and friends.

❷ Talk about how the water in the pool would sometimes stir up and ripple. Families and friends would help their sick friend down into the water because they believed that the first person in the pool after the water stirred would be healed and made better of whatever illness he/she had.

❸ Jesus came to the pool one Sabbath day, (like a Sunday) and he saw the man who had been ill for many years sitting alone. Jesus asked him, "Do you want to get better?"

❹ Continue the story in your own words right to the end of verse 9. Don't get involved with the Jewish authorities' arguments concerning the Sabbath but do explain how Jesus met the man again, this time in the temple (verse 14), and their conversation.

✎ *Notes*

BOOK 3 UNIT 10

Activity Sheet – Beside the Pool

The man who walks and runs

Prepare in advance
❶ Cut out a cardboard template of the man and use it to cut out the required number of men in white card.
❷ Cut out a cardboard template of rotating feet.
❸ Cut out in cereal packet card circles with a 4cm radius.
❹ Draw rotating feet onto each circle using the template.
❺ Using a bradawl make a hole in the bottom of the man's coat and in the centre of the circle.

You will need
☆ white card: 1 A2 sheet makes 8 men
☆ old cereal packets
☆ crayons
☆ split pins
☆ bradawl (or something with a sharp point)
☆ pencils

What each child/parent does
❶ Colour in the man's face, hair, hands, clothes etc.
❷ Draw feet and sandals on the circles.

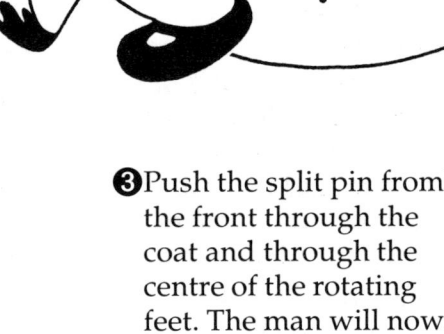

❸ Push the split pin from the front through the coat and through the centre of the rotating feet. The man will now walk and run if you push him along.

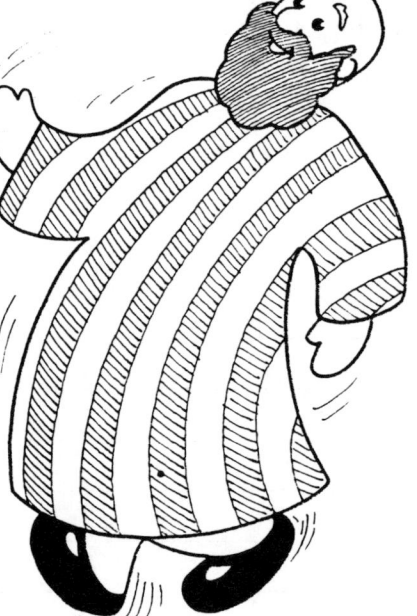

Get the room ready
Put out for each child/parent:
• 1 man
• 1 circle
• 1 split pin
Put out on the table:
• crayons
• pencils

Bibliography

Songlist

Big Man JP 16 (7); **Come into his presence** (6); **Everyone matters to Jesus** SHKP3 (7); **God is for me, though I am little** CH 100 (1) (2) (5); **God is good, we sing and shout it** JP 55 (7); **God knows me and you** (7); **God loves you and I love you** (7); **God's love is like a circle** (5); **Have you seen the pussy cat?** JP 72 (5); **I have hand**s (4); **Jesus' hands are kind hands** JP 134 (4); **Jesus, Jesus here I am** (7) (8); **Jesus' love is a powerful love** (7) (8); **Jesus' love is very wonderful** JP 139 (2); **Lord, we come to worship you** SFLT 28 (3); **Lord you gave me joy in my heart** SFLT 27 (3) (8); **My God is so big, so strong and so mighty** JP 169 (2) (5); **Peter, James and John in a sailboat** JP 198 (5); **Who's that sitting in a sycamore tree?** (4); **Who's the king of the jungle?** JP 289 (2) (5); **You can weigh an elephant's auntie** (7); **Zacchaeus was a very little man** JP 300

CH = Cry Hosanna
JP = Junior Praise
SFLT - Ishmael's Songs for Little Troopers
SHKP - Kids' Praise Spring Harvest 1990 (Uncage the Lion)
(1) = God is for Me - cassette by the Fisherfolk (Celebration Tapes - CT 22032)
(2) = Sing to the King - Richard and Sue Sutton and Linda Grant, 10 Wellington Road, St Albans, AL1 5NI
(3) = Ishmael's Songs for Little Troopers - cassette Songs of Fellowship/Kingsway SFC 212
(4) = Jesus Loves Me - the Keynotes, St John's Harbourne (available through CPAS)
(5) = Praise You, Lord - the Keynotes, St John's Harbourne (available through CPAS)
(6) = Praise Him - cassette Integrity Music Just For Kids IMK 002 (available through Word UK)
(7) = Everyone Matters to Jesus - the Keynotes, St John's Harbourne (available through CPAS)
(8) = Kids' Praise, Spring Harvest 1988 (distributed by ICC)

Booklist

The Palm Tree Bible - The Wonderful Stories of Jesus from the New Testament, Book 1 (formerly Good News from Jesus), Palm Tree Press 1989; *The Lion Book of Bible Stories and Prayers*, Lion Publishing 1980; *The Lion Book of Stories of Jesus*, Lion Publishing 1986; *Cry Hosanna*, Betty Pulkingham/Mimi Fara, Hodder and Stoughton 1980; *Ishmael's Songs for Little Troopers*, Ishmael, Kingsway Music 1990; *Junior Praise*, Marshall Pickering 1986; *Kid's Praise Spring Harvest 1990* (Uncage the Lion), ICC 1990; *Round and Round the Garden*, Sarah Williams, Oxford University Press 1983

Resources and addresses

Glove Puppet Kits, Celebration Arts, PO Box 68, Redhill, Surrey, RH1 4YT
Help I Can't Draw, Books 1,2,3, available through CPAS
Under Fives Welcome! Kathleen Crawford, Scripture Union 1990
Under Fives and their Families, A CPAS Handbook, Judith Wigley, Marshall Pickering 1990
Telling Stories to Children, Marshall Shelley, Lion Publishing 1990
Makaton Vocabulary Development Project, Mrs Margaret Walker, 31 Firwood Drive, Camberley, Surrey
Celebrating the Festivals, Bible Stories and Activities with the under fives, Book 1, Sue Kirby, available through CPAS
Stories Jesus Told, Bible Stories and Activities with the under fives, Book 2, Sue Kirby, available through CPAS

Text © 1991 Sue Kirby
This edition © 1991 CPAS

Published by
Church Pastoral Aid Society
Athena Drive
Tachbrook Park
Warwick
CV34 6NG

First edition 1991
ISBN 0 9077 5071 0

All rights reserved
The templates in each book may be photocopied for use with groups of up to ten children

Line drawings reproduced on page 12 are used with the kind permission of
Makaton Vocabulary Development Project
31 Firwood Drive
Camberley Surrey

Editorial, design, typesetting and production by
AD Publishing Services Ltd
0296 434553/661273

Cover illustration by
Christine Garlick

Printed by City Print
(Milton Keynes) Ltd